T0365426

GOD,
WHY
AM I DIFFERENT?

*A Workbook Dedicated to the Introduction of **God's** Creation of the World and How He Creates Everyone Special*

Author: Kathy Wines

Illustrations by Derek Wines

Copyright © 2021 Kathy Wines.

All rights reserved. No part of this book may be used or reproduced by any means, graphic, electronic, or mechanical, including photocopying, recording, taping or by any information storage retrieval system without the written permission of the author except in the case of brief quotations embodied in critical articles and reviews.

WestBow Press books may be ordered through booksellers or by contacting:

WestBow Press
A Division of Thomas Nelson & Zondervan
1663 Liberty Drive
Bloomington, IN 47403
www.westbowpress.com
844-714-3454

Because of the dynamic nature of the Internet, any web addresses or links contained in this book may have changed since publication and may no longer be valid. The views expressed in this work are solely those of the author and do not necessarily reflect the views of the publisher, and the publisher hereby disclaims any responsibility for them.

Any people depicted in stock imagery provided by Getty Images are models, and such images are being used for illustrative purposes only. Certain stock imagery © Getty Images.

Illustrations by Derek Wines

Scriptures quotations are taken from the International Children's Bible®, copyright ©1986, 1988, 1999, 2015 by Tommy Nelson. Used by permission.

ISBN: 978-1-6642-1851-2 (sc)
ISBN: 978-1-6642-1852-9 (e)

Library of Congress Control Number: 2021906961

Print information available on the last page.

WestBow Press rev. date: 04/07/2021

WESTBOW
PRESS®
A DIVISION OF THOMAS NELSON
& ZONDERVAN

KATHY'S PURPOSE

As a mother, blessed to have a son with Autism, providing the understanding of God's wonders has always been a challenge.

Children are our blessings, and of course, we are all God's children. My goal is to honor our Lord by assuring that regardless of any disability, physical or emotional, we are all made perfectly by God.

This workbook is a Christian study guide that begins with the elementary introduction to **God** and his marvelous creation of the world, His power and love for His children and ends by tying it to an introduction to the Bible – God's Word.

This workbook can be used in Sunday School, Bible School, homeschool or developing a devotional time for young people.

Prayer:

Dear **God**, Thank you for your wonderful creation of the whole world and your unconditional love for each of us. Open our eyes and hearts to understand that all of us were created entirely by you. Amen

Table of Contents

WELCOME!

I am thrilled that you and I are going to be spending some time together to learn about **Gods** fantastic creation and to explore our question "**God**, Why Am I different?

I pinky promise you will like the answer!

INSTRUCTIONS

This workbook is a fun activity for you to do with your family, friends, teacher or in a group setting, getting to know how much **God** loves you.

Dear Reader:

You will need the following:

1. Pen or Pencil
2. Red pencil or pen. Each time you see the word God circle his name with a red pencil or pen.
3. Crayons or colored pencils/markers.
4. Tape or Glue
5. Two pictures: One photo of you and one of someone you love.
6. Bible: Paper copy or computer app.

ARE YOUR READY? I AM!

Part 1:

God Did What? OH MY!!!

Workbook Activity:

Take the next few minutes and close your eyes and remember some of the things you did over the past six days.

Please write down six things you have done over the past six days.

1. _____

2. _____

3. _____

4. _____

5. _____

6. _____

You did a lot!

Place a checkmark by your favorite!

<u>Next Page:</u> MEET GOD!

Let's look at how God spent His six days!
Check out His list!

God creates the sky and the Earth!

Day One:

....

God spoke: "Let there be light", And there was light.". God named the light "day" and the darkness "night". Evening passed, and morning came. This was the first day."[1]

Let's take a moment to think about day and night.

Every day since then, we have had a day and night. It never changes! It is something that **God** made for us!

God created our world's first day!!

Day Two:

....

The second day **God** spoke: "Let there be something to divide the water in two"! So, God made the air to divide the water in two. Some of the water was above the air and some of the water was below it. God named the air "sky."[2]

Did you notice that God just spoke the words, and it happened!! That is a big WOW!

Workbook Activity:

1. Underline the word spoke in both days.
2. Using a red pencil or pen circle every time we mentioned **God** on this page.

---

[1] (Genesis 1:1-5)
[2] (Genesis 1:6-8)

Day Three:

On the third day, **God** spoke, "let the water under the sky be gathered together so the dry land will appear." And it happened. **God** named the dry land "earth", and He named the water the "seas". God saw that this was good. On this day **God** made the land earth and the oceans![3]

God made the oceans! Remember, **God** created the Earth, and now he is designing the oceans to separate the land on Earth.

Workbook Activity:

1. Underline the word spoke.

2. Can you name the five Oceans?

   1. Atlantic Ocean

   2. Pacific Ocean

   3. Indian Ocean

   4. Antarctic Ocean

   5. Arctic Ocean

3. Have you ever been to the ocean? Circle: Yes or No

4. Which ocean is closest to your house?

5. Using a red pencil or pen circle every time we mentioned God on this page.

[3] (Genesis 1:9-13)

NEXT:

Then **God** spoke, "Let the Earth produce plants. Some plants will make grain for seeds. Others will make fruit with seeds in it. Every seed will produce more of its own kind of plant."[4]

Fun Fact:

There are at least 7,500 different apples in the world! *

That's a lot of different apples!

Workbook Activity:

1. Underline the word <u>spoke.</u>
2. Using a red pencil or pen circle every time we mentioned <u>God</u> on this page.

*According to: https://web.extension.illinois.edu/apples/facts.cfm

Workbook Activity:

Write down your favorite two fruits that God made for you!

1. _____

2. _____

_____
[4] (Genesis 1:9-13)

Draw your favorite fruits below:

Day Four

On the fourth day, **God** spoke: <u>"Let there be lights in the sky to separate the day from night. These lights will be used for signs, seasons, days and years."</u>[5]

Can you guess what **God** put in the sky? Stars!

Workbook Activity:

1. Underline the word <u>spoke.</u>
2. Using a red pencil or pen circle every time we mentioned **<u>God</u>** on this page.

---

[5] (Genesis 1:14-19)

3. Draw a few stars on this page, make each of them different!

Next time you are outside at night look up and see how many stars **God** made in the sky!

Maybe just for fun you can look up and see how many you can count!

Fun Fact:

No person knows exactly how many stars are in the sky. However, **God** knows exactly how many stars He created in the Universe! Did you know that the sun is a star?

Just think **God** made all those stars different and special!

Sun and the Moon

On the fourth day, **God** also wanted us to be able to see outside at night and during the day, so he made the sun and the moon!

Fun Facts:

The sun is about 865,000 miles across, and it is so large that God could put our Earth inside it over a million times! **WOW!**

The Earth is almost 4,000 miles across the middle, and over 25,000 miles around the equator. The moon is about 1,000 miles across the center.

Now take one moment to think about those fun facts. **God** created those stars so we can see to live here on Earth!

Workbook Activity:

1. Using a red pencil or pen circle every time we mentioned **<u>God</u>** on this page.

Lesson Four

Day Five

On the fifth day of creation, **God** spoke <u>"Let the water be filled with living things. And let birds fly in the air above the Earth. God created the large animals…. God also made every bird that flies…"</u>[6]

On this day it is shared in the Bible that **God** created the big sea mammals. Whales are big! Remember, **God** <u>made each of the sea mammals **different**</u>.

*Fun Fact: 1) The biggest whale in the ocean is the blue whale, and it can weigh more than 150 tons and measure over 100 ft long. 2) The blue whale is known to be the largest mammal living. 3) These great big whales only eat krill! Krill look like shrimp.

*<u>WWW.whalefacts.org</u>

Workbook Activity:

Let's have a little math fun!

1. **Question:** How many pounds does a blue whale weigh? The Blue whale can weigh over 150 tons.

One ton equals 2000 pounds

<u>Multiply:</u>

2000 pounds x 150 tons

Answer: The **blue whale** can weigh 300,000 pounds! That's big!

------

[6] (Genesis 1:20-23)

How much do you weigh?_____

2.   Using a red pencil or pen circle every time we mentioned **God** on this page.

Let's think here for a moment: **God** created the oceans first so that this giant whale could live in it, but **God** also created lots of other fish in the sea. He made them all different species and each of them with different colors, eyes in places that may make them look strange and the ability to live underwater!!! WOW

God created the birds:

God created many different species of birds.

He made them with wings so they can fly!!!! Look at their little legs and how beautiful their wings are colored.

Workbook Activity:

Look outside the window.   What is your favorite bird?

1.   Can you draw a picture of a bird?

2.   Using a red pencil or pen circle every time we mentioned **<u>God</u>** on this page.

God spoke "Let the Earth be filled with animals. And let each produce more of its own kind. Let there be tame animals and small crawling animals and wild animals. And let each produce more of its kind."[7]

Animal fun

Male African elephants are the largest of all land animals and can weigh an average of 5 tons. That means 36 elephants weigh as much as the Blue whale **God** created on day five! **God** sure can-do big things when he wants too! *

Workbook Activity:

1. Underline the word spoke.
2. Using a red pencil or pen circle every time we mentioned **God** on this page.

*www.livescience.com

---
[7] (Genesis 1:24)

What is your favorite animal? Just think, **God** created all the animals!

1. _____

1. _____

1. _____

God Creates Man and Woman!

God made the first two people to live on Earth. He first made man, and then he made the first woman. Their names were Adam and Eve.

They lived in the most beautiful place on Earth, and it was called the Garden of Eden. It was a perfect place with beautiful flowers, trees, fruit and lots of animals![8]

---

[8] (Genesis: 1,2)

God declared the seventh day as a day of rest.[9]
You know this day as Sunday.

Prayer is how we communicate with God

Please read and say out loud the prayer of the day below:

Prayer for Today:

Dear **God**, Thank you for all the fantastic creations of the world. Thank you for wanting me to be a part of Your world that you designed. Thank you for creating Earth, the moon, sun and stars. Thank you for making all the animals. Help me, God, always remember that I live on the Earth You created for all of your people. Amen

---

[9] (Genesis: 2:1-3)

Part 1 Review

Did you notice on each day God spoke his creation?

Fill in the blank: Name one thing God created on each day.

Day One **God** created _____

Day Two **God** created _____

Day Three **God** created _____

Day Four **God** created _____

Day Five **God** created _____

Day Six **God** created _____

What did **God** do on the Seventh Day? _____

Question: Did God create everything the same or different? Circle your answer.

    a.   Same

    b.   Different

Answer: (b) **God** created everything differently!

Part 2:

God, You and the Superheroes!

Can you guess who else **God** has made?

God made You and me!

Out of all the things **GOD** made, people are the most important. We are all **God's** children.

Just think **God** made you!

Workbook Activity:

It's time to paste or glue your picture below. If you do not have a picture, you can draw a picture of yourself!

Do you know who Godzilla is in the movies?

He is the king of all the monsters in the whole world!

Just for fun, can you draw your favorite make-believe monster?

He is strong and can fly!

Workbook Activity:

Just for fun again, use your biggest imagination and draw your favorite superhero or cartoon hero. Write down your characters favorite powers!

_____

_____

Make-believe stories are fun, they they make us laugh or just entertain us. We must always understand what is real and what is pretend. Superheroes and monsters are pretend.

I am very excited to share with you the next part about **<u>God</u>**!

Now we need to learn what is correct, now and always!

<u>God</u> is the King!

<u>God</u> is a real King!

<u>God</u> is the ONLY King of the Universe!

*** Using a red pencil or pen circle every time we mentioned **<u>God</u>** on this page. ***

God is more powerful than Godzilla, all his monsters and all the superheroes put together!!!

Are you ready for some awesome news?

God has real superpowers because **God** is real!

God makes the sun shine!

God makes it rain and snow!

God makes the flowers bloom!

Draw a heart here:

Fill in the blank with the word "me".

<u>God</u> loves_____always and forever.

<u>God</u> can hear_____anytime and anywhere.

I am never alone. <u>God</u> is always with_____.

<u>God</u> made you just the way he wanted you to be! You are perfect in <u>God's</u> eyes.

Write below: <u>God</u> loves me forever

Write your name <u>in the heart</u> on the previous page.

God is the only real **God** of the Universe!

Fill in the blanks: (write God)

_____ is the only King of the Universe.

_____ created me perfect in His eyes.

_____ loves me with all His heart FOREVER.

_____ is good.

Please read and say out loud the prayer of the day below:

Prayer for Today:

Thank you, Dear **God,** for loving me always and forever! Amen

Lesson Eight

Your Birthday!

God designed you before you were born!

Did you know that your birthday is your special day?
Your birthday is the day that **God** brought you into the world!

Workbook Activity:

When is your birthday?

Write the date below please:

_____

On the next blank page draw a picture of what you like to do on your birthday to celebrate!

Draw here:

You were brought into this world because **<u>God</u>** loves you.

Take time to share how you like to celebrate with your friends and family. Find out what they want to do on their birthday too.

?

GOD, WHY AM I DIFFERENT?

GOD MADE EVERY PERSON DIFFERENT AND SPECIAL!

Let's take a minute to remember all of the **different** things that **God** created!

Circle all the things that God created different and special:

Workbook Activity:

Land Animals   **Flowers**

Stars   **Trees**

Birds   **People**

Do you remember what happened on the 6th day of God's creation?

God created the first man and woman, Adam and Eve. They were different from each other.

Adam was the first man. **God** created him over 6000 years ago!

And then **God** made a woman named Eve. They lived in a perfect place with **God** called the Garden of Eden.

Adam and Eve were the first people **God** created. God created all people differently.

Draw a picture below of someone in your family or a friend.

Can you list below how the person in your picture is different from you?

1.

2.

3.

Can you imagine what our world would be like if we all looked and acted the same?

We would not know who was who!

That would be silly!!!!

Please read and say out loud the prayer of the day below:

Prayer for Today:

Thank you, **<u>God</u>**, for making me special and different! Amen

You are special!

Today we are going to see how special God created all of us. In the last lesson, we learned that **God** made all of us different. He decided everything about you before you were even born!

Workbook Activity:

Fill in the blanks about you:

Color of eyes: _____

Color of hair: _____

Color of skin: _____

Fun fact: There have been more than 107 billion people God created, and not one person was identical to another person.

Remember, **<u>God</u>** is perfect and cannot make a mistake, not now or ever.

When we look around, we see people who look different:

Some people use crutches.

Some people wear special shoes.

Some people get to ride in a wheelchair.

Some people have speech problems.

Some people cannot see or hear.

Our looks are one thing that makes us different, but many other parts of us make us special, unique and different.

Examples of what makes me different, special and unique:

I like spinach pizza and chocolate cake.

I do not like tomatoes.

I like football.

I do not like soccer.

I like friendly people.

I cannot sing.

List or draw below some things that you like and dislike:

Everyone shares the love in their heart differently!

This is the most important part of you. This is what God sees in you![10]

1)   How do you show your <u>kindness</u> to others?

2)   Give an example of how you like to <u>help</u> other people:

3)   Give an example of how you <u>love</u> someone.

4)   What do you like to <u>share</u>?

---

[10] (Ephesians 2:10)

God knows all of the following about you.[11]

Copy each of the statements below:

1) **God** knows "all about me".

2) **God** knows "when I sit down and I get up".

3) **God** knows "my thoughts before I think them".

4) **God** knows "everything I do".

5) **God** is always with me.

6) **God** knows "more than I can understand".

---

[11] (Psalms 139:1-6).

One more time! Read and say out loud!

One important difference is what is in your heart.

The way you **love** people.

The way you **care** about your family and friends.

The way you **care** and **love** your animals.

Always remember that **<u>God</u>** loves you and that you should always love Him.

Please read and say out loud the prayer of the day below:

Prayer for Today:

Dear **God**, thank you for making me just the way you wanted me to be on Earth. Thank you for making each of us different, just like you made every star in the sky different. Amen

LOVE, LOVE and MORE LOVE!

Our question we have been answering is God, Why Am I Different? Our answer has been clearly, God is so awesome that he makes everything different. Nothing is the same.

Here is the other part of our answer. He made everyone different because:

****

He created us different because He <u>loves</u> each of us and wants to have a relationship with each of us. He knows each of us and wants us to know Him!

In Part 3 of our book, we will discover how we all can know who God is, what He wants for us and how he wants us to live our lives.

****

You are special – just the way **God** wanted you to be! He loves us so much He created us in His image! [12] You look, think and act just the way **God** made you!

God has given everyone a very special gift. **LOVE**

Now that is good news!!

---

[12] Genesis 1:27)

Love is a gift from God[13]

When you go to school and study, you get a grade that you earned. That is not a gift; you earned the grade. If you receive an allowance for doing chores at your house, you earned money. It is not a gift.

If someone hands you a present it is a gift, perhaps for your birthday it is not because you did something but because they care about you. You did not earn it.

God gives us a gift, love.

Read out loud the following statements:

God's love is a free gift from God!

God never makes mistakes because **God** is perfect.

God loves me now and forever.

---

[13] (Ephesians 2:8-9)

God wants us to love Him the most.

God loves everyone the same amount.

There is only one **God.**

God never runs out of love for me!

Please read and say out loud the prayer of the day below:

Prayer for Today:

Thank you, **God,** for giving me the gift of love. Amen

Part 3:

PACK YOUR BACKPACK – THE BUS IS READY TO GO!

Field Trip!

Let's all get on the bus and discover the Bible!

Workbook Activity:

Feel free to draw a bus for our trip!

The Bible is God's Book, and it is all TRUE!

There are ___5___ learning points at this stop. This is important!

1.   The Bible is "God's Word" – it is the way God speaks to all of us.

2.   The Bible is the way we learn about God.

3.   The Bible teaches us about how God led His people a long time ago.

4.   Reading God's written Word in the Bible is how God guides us through our lives.

5.   We speak to God by praying anytime and anywhere we want to pray.

Workbook Activity:

Circle the correct statement.

a.   The Bible is God's Word.

b.   The Bible is the way we learn about God.

c.   The Bible teaches us about how God led His people a long time ago.

d.   Reading God's written Word in the Bible is how God guides us through our lives.

e.   We speak to God by praying, anytime, anywhere we want to pray.

Answer: all of them are correct

Let's explore how God wrote the Bible:

Have you ever asked someone to write down something for you?

Workbook Activity:

1) Ask someone you know to write something down just as you would like it written. It can be a short sentence or a funny thought. Make it easy, please.

2) Tell someone about something you have seen yesterday or today. Now ask them to write it.

Keep it simple.

Now you have something written without you writing it down, but it is your words on the paper and your story that you wanted to share.

God wrote the Bible without Him ever actually writing anything with a pen.

God told special people what to write.

God had people write many stories about people and events that took place many years ago.

All the writing was done to teach us how much God loves us and how we are supposed to live our lives. His goal is for us to live in Heaven with Him for Eternity.

SECOND STOP

The Bible

When was the earliest part of the Bible written?

Answer: A man named Moses wrote the first parts of the Bible for God. He wrote his part of the Bible about 3500 years ago. A LONG TIME AGO!

The Bible is God's Word. IT IS ALL TRUE. Please read that again and underline those two short sentences. God has done and continues to do many miraculous and beautiful things for everyone every day.

Everyone should spend their entire life reading and learning what God says in the Bible, so we can live our lives the way he wants us to live every day.

Have you ever been to a swimming pool? Draw a swimming pool below.

The first thing you may do is put your toes in it to see if it's cold or warm. Then if the temperature of the water is ok, you can get in and enjoy the water. You can go a little deeper.

That is how we are going to begin studying the Bible. We are going to put our toes in just enough for you find out how beautiful Gods Word is written in the Bible so you will want to learn more (or if you were swimming, you would go deeper in the water).

THIRD STOP

On this stop, we will explore the following question: **What's the Bible teaching us?** Get your pencil out!

Workbook Activity:

Can you write two things you believe the Bible is about in the space below? (I will give you a hint – you have already learned at least two things in this workbook!)

1. <u>God</u> created _____

2. <u>God</u> loves _____

3. <u>God</u> made everyone _____

Answers: 1. Everything – you can list anything. 2. me, 3. different

Underline with colored pencil or ink each time you read below: <u>Gods</u> Word in the Bible says:

1. <u>God's</u> Word in the Bible says: <u>God</u> knew you before you were born! (Jeremiah 1:4-5)

2. <u>God's</u> Word in the Bible says: we are <u>Gods</u> special creation. (Ephesians: 2:10)

3. <u>God's</u> Word in the Bible says: <u>God</u> created us the way He wants us to be and for God's purpose. (Colossians 1:16)

Circle in line 1: (Jeremiah 1:4-5)

Circle in line 2: (Ephesians: 2:10)

Circle in line 3: (Colossians 1:16)

Great work!

You have now just circled three places in the Bible that <u>God</u> talked about how wonderfully He created you!

Now write below: The Bible is all true.

_____

_____

_____

_____

_____

_____

_____

_____

_____

_____

Do you remember the Big question we started within this workbook?

GOD, WHY AM I DIFFERENT?

BIG ANSWER:

GOD MADE ALL PEOPLE DIFFERENT AND SPECIAL BECAUSE HE LOVES US!

You know this is true!

The Bible says it is true!

You are special and
loved by God!

It's time to get on the bus and head home. Thank you for traveling with me.

My note to each of you!

Remember:

God will always be with you and love you.

Thank you for taking the time to spend with me as we explored the basics of God's creation of the world. We discovered all people are different and special, just as God designed us because He loves each of us. We took a look at the best book ever written, The Holy Bible. I hope you will continue with me on the journey to develop a personal relationship with God and discover all he has done for us.

God Bless All of You,
Kathy

Acknowledgment

I would like to first and foremost thank God for trusting our family with Derek. He has brought immeasurable love to all of our lives. He has taught us to appreciate the "normal" of life through his eyes. His innocence and compassion for others have been an inspiration in our family.

I want to thank my husband, Billy and all of my family for their continued love and support.

I want to also thank Pastor Tommy Bridges for his inspiring sermon that led me to see my purpose in writing this workbook, and his wife, who I am privileged to call a friend, Chaplain Lynn Bridges, for her continued support in writing this book. I would also like to give a special thanks to my cousin Lee Isaacson and his wife, Pastor Maggie Isaacson, for their love and support.

And a big thanks to Derek for drawing the pictures for this workbook!

Special note: I would like to thank everyone in advance for offering only positive comments on any illustrations in this book. Derek lives with Autism and strives to do his best, and the pictures are his best. Thank you.

GOD,
WHY
AM I DIFFERENT?

Printed in the United States
by Baker & Taylor Publisher Services